do not be lulled by the dainty starlike blossom

Poems by Rachael Matthews

For my beloved Jean and Eleanor

☙

'Poetry can break open locked chambers of possibility, restore numbed zones to feeling, recharge desire.'
Adrienne Rich

THE EMMA PRESS

First published in the UK in 2021 by The Emma Press Ltd.
Poems © Rachael Matthews 2021.

All rights reserved.

The right of Rachael Matthews to be identified as the author of this work has been asserted in accordance with the Copyright, Designs and Patents Act 1988.

ISBN 978-1-912915-81-1

A CIP catalogue record of this book
is available from the British Library.

Printed and bound in the UK
by Oxuniprint, Oxford.

The Emma Press
theemmapress.com
hello@theemmapress.com
Birmingham, UK

CONTENTS

do not be lulled by the dainty starlike blossom 1
birthmark 2
Birthday party 3
The ride 4
Hinterland 5
family circus 6
suddenly 7
Swimming pool 8
The Lark Ascending 9
Ghazal: the sea 10
Ventriloquism 11
Portion controlled dinner for my love, Yitzhak 12
Mrs Arnolfini's interior 14
Daffodils 15
Frozen dream 16
chicken 18
frozen embryo: 19
undead as a girl 20
Finding Rapa Nui on Google Earth (May, 2020) 21
Confinement 23
recovery 24
settled 25
ultrasound / ego gravida 26
free association 27

Acknowledgements 29
About the poet 30
About The Emma Press 30

do not be lulled by the dainty starlike blossom

at the radiance tea house on 55th
we watch jasmine pearls unfold in our cups
meaty labial   aroused
i tell you two stories about shame and rage:

there was no dinner for a week
after i mentioned liking girls
so i rode my bike to the jasmine takeaway
with stolen money and stared at koi carp
and a picture of a chinese river from above
while my chips were cooked—
quickly & without any shouting or crying—
and when the owner came with my food
i was so ready for punishment i thought
her *thank you* sounded like *fuck you*

on a wooden table that widened
for christmas and collapsed for new year
i was told to eat until i could see the river
with the two people in conical hats
standing on a bridge at the bottom
of my blue bowl—the only one safe enough
to touch with my favourite spoon—
tricked every time into seconds
"and what do you say to your father?"
my *fuck you* sounded like *thank you*

birthmark

born without a mark on her was the popular myth conceived about me by one parent who knew the value of a blemish-free start and the other who knew the inevitability of gradual defects like the pink thumb print on the nape of my neck that emerged sometime between hairlessness and the time I cut the long locks that followed me around for years keeping me anchored to the wishes of one parent for a girl who could be combed and the demands of another for a girl who could serve as proof that something clean could come of his own imperfections and in realizing this much later I pursued all things unsullied such as white sand and snow laden only with itself and not unlike the page upon blank page of a writing book fronted by a spotless rose that one parent gave me to fill with lines she dare not dream of and the other could never conceive of and which remains blank to this day because there are no words that belong in between the sheets of such a quest for perfection by proxy

Birthday party

I bring a card with stitched-on tactile dinosaur
saying THREE TODAY in twenty-point Comic Sans.
Before torn paper and red cake
my brother shows me around like an estate agent:
due to instead of *because*. It's a language on loan
and he seems glad to have it after months on mute.
I do what he wants: praise the sterile new rooms of his house
remembering how he sledgehammered them dead
on broken news of our mother's *exit strategy,*
what he calls *that stunt with a knife.*
His taut wife beckons me, fiddling with bunting.
You have to do something—
he keeps cleaning things, won't let me breathe,
goes to bed with a headache thinking it's the end.
Through a doorway I watch him with his son—
blue-eyed, blond, the same-shaped head.

The ride

Driving back from the rollercoaster
we're lulled by our level progress,
talked out from reliving the second dip
much bigger than the first and more sudden.

This time our mother tipped and slid
within a week. Began rattling inside
the carriage of her own bones.

So we send gifts and visit.
My brother brings his kids,
holds up the new baby like a prize.

While she sleeps we escape,
try to laugh at the fairground but fail
until we find hilarity in sudden free fall.

Driving back from the rollercoaster
my brother whispers over his shoulder
you're quiet, what are you thinking about?
checking whether five-year-olds
get lost in dark tunnels too.

Godzilla says a voice slack with distraction.
We draw up outside her house;
at first nobody moves to get out.

Hinterland

Out past the orange windsock,
the old gasworks, the static
caravan lot, the graves start.
This wide place has a future,
is growing rows. We flock there
in black carrying N-A-N
and M-U-M in too-bright blooms.
My brother's anxious about
the pregnancy. His unborn son's
baptism shawl erratic, unpicked,
the first sign she wasn't well;
my uncle in his civil service shoes
is bringing something of the Cenotaph;
my aunt more poised since
her divorce is watching my mother's
laugh-cries and medication shake.
Her bingo friends nod, hang back
while my soft slow cousin sobs
in mirror shades and Nikes.
I mull a collective noun for mourners,
reject lament and sorrow,
choose murmuration—
all those starlings she'd shoo away.

family circus

because my mother's a frayed thread
in a long line of circus acts
i'd have to sit near the ring
getting spotlit when the clown got close
his name burlesque—something ending in 'o'
on a bill crowned by a lion
you could hear before you could see
like the spring and the shark in jaws
he'd haunch into the room sawdust-footed
while breaths were pulled in
fearing at the very least a flash of teeth
while someone else was juggling things
and bound to fail sooner or later
like the skittish animal trainer
little more than a craw full of flesh
with too flimsy a whip
and me the sword swallower
keeping everything down
forever thinking to myself
this shouldn't go on indoors

suddenly

i'm sitting on the doorstop in mickey mouse shades
half indoors half out holding my own hands
scented with tennis balls and tarmac

the sun-charged surface of my cul-de-sac
where suddenly this summer i can only pretend to play
after a cornering with no sharp exits to be had

my outgrown cotton top with printed-on cartoon cop
warning *one false move!* is all the power that i have
except my cowboy pistol's bloodless *pop!*

Swimming pool

Deep down we all knew something was buried.
Julie whose made-up mum went out at midnight
tried to dig it up one day along with Gail
who'd just got new parents and a bike
that braked when you pedalled backwards.
We took plastic spades to the bare patch
between our sapling goal posts. Summer had cracked
its surface, making us suddenly ambitious—
even the ice cream van came and went unseen.
Julie's brother arrived barefoot carrying a lolly
shaped like a space rocket and sat cross-legged
beside the six-inch hole. He said we needed water
for softening and returned with a small bucket
slopping over. The pouring was solemn
and drew Jason whose dad had been gone since Christmas.
The water bubbled in, sat there, then sank
leaving the smell after rain and all the promise of a tunnel
to the filled-in swimming pool with its cool blue tiles,
easy shallows, deep end, and the ladder out.

The Lark Ascending

The Lark Ascending came home on cassette,
scarred by a sliding life on the library's music racks.
Inside, a thin sleeve with a Constable scene, some clouds,
a rainbow, but no larks. Gummed to the case, stuck askew,
a paper record of borrowed days stamped in green.
March 4th 1981—the year my mother pressed play
and put the whole house on pause. Maybe even the street.
There was a bit-by-bit beginning, a guttering start,
as if this bird I'd never seen or heard was testing itself;
finding the steady melody of something sure of song.
Then the lark began flirting with falling, rooting me to the spot.
I watched my mother smile—lids shut, head inclined.
When the lark disappeared she opened her eyes
as if to check she still had sight. *That's twenty pence well-spent*
she said, sighing all thoughts of the lark into the fridge.
Your father will be home soon and just look at me.
Years later I go to Carnegie Hall to hear each note
learned in the strip-lit kitchen played out in front of me
and the shock is not the sound but the sight of the violinist
shutting her eyes at the same lines that made my mother close hers
and I wonder why mine are still so completely and utterly open.

Ghazal: the sea

I was raised by the ocean but never swam because
>my mother couldn't stand the sea.
The fucking sea, she would say, *cold and grey and endless,*
>meaning her marriage not the sea.

My father went out with the lifeboat. He was all about
>the storm. Sou'westers and force ten gales.
He taught me the necessity / futility of rescue and put-on
>masculinity, disguised as a story about the sea.

I live in the city now. My lover explains why the tides
>turn twice a day, why there has to be a low ebb.
Summer weekends we go to the shore to be shocked /
>lullabied by the pull and promise of the sea.

I don't fear the water, but its undertow. My heels dig deep,
>past-leaning. Hers spring forward, clock-like.
She collects black shells. They go grey overnight. They/she
>are more themselves in the sea.

I'm not getting in. I'm scared. *If you loved me,* she'd say,
>*if you loved me you'd brave the sea.*
Start again. Go all the way back. Re-name. Say
>*having a child* every time you hear: *the sea.*

Ventriloquism

Sundays she hands me the weddings section
like a saved dessert. After property, investments,
mergers and acquisitions, she wants skin touch
and stories made from smiling headshots. Side by side
in yesterday's underwear, in the pressed-in middle
of the sofa, she noses my hair, closes her eyes, wants it
to start. I always do it the same: couples like us,
couples not like us, the feature pair with the photo shoot
then the older two who're unlikely—have known pain
that's similar but different. I tell her that Jennifer and Ruth
were married Saturday in Brooklyn and have Master's degrees.
She wants me to say they won't last, so I do; I even
use the word doomed and rhyme their new surname
with cannoli in a voice I never knew I had. I tell her
that Ryan and Paige are Harvard magna cum laudes
but now work as Elmos in Times Square. She's laughing
and still with the red fur and the ping-pong ball eyes
when I switch to straight-faced for Kirsten and Brad
who met at spin class. The couple's first date was lunch
at the Starlight Diner, I report next. She's already hooked
because we go there ourselves and know romance.
Kirsten had the reuben, Brad the turkey club, I lie delicately.
Because she's become immune to pointless detail
she thinks it's verbatim. I end on Bill and Marcia,
forced by death onto Match.com. Even though his banking
and her non-profit seemed at odds they connected through jazz;
a friend of the bride officiated; Marcia is keeping her name.
She takes hold of the paper, looks at their newlove faces,
pronounces them perfect. What is magna cum laude I ask her,
thinking of champagne and Chaucer. Just like after sex
she slides off me and onto her phone. Second-best
I say, after googling it first. Why brag about that, she wonders.

Portion controlled dinner for my love, Yitzhak

Digital image, 2016

On my Facebook feed a chicken thigh
resting on a plate of yellow rice

the close-up quality of amateur porn.
Your grandmother Ruth is holding up

the meal like her firstborn. Proud and
tired from labour. The drumstick

mirrors her bony thumb gripping
her prized Dutch blue porcelain.

I think Vermeer: *Woman with a Fowl.*
Ruth's eyes are kind because of the skin

that half-hoods them. The same skin
her friend Elaine recently had cut back

like a circumcision. I start to imagine Yitzhak
eating the meal: Ruth slicing up the meat,

feeding him, rice dropping. The two of them
on the bed remembering cruises, Murano glass,

the little landscape from Bermuda with
its ever-cresting wave. The phone will ring,

he'll think it's Mensa; she'll think it's
their eldest daughter or Carnegie Hall.

I see Ruth in the kitchen uploading her photo,
titling it & waiting for likes. Comments come

mostly on his bravery and her new hair, but then
cage-free hens, colons, and Donald Trump.

I call you over to see. I never want to live
like that, you tell me. Like what, I ask.

In a one-sided way with one of us sicker,
out of sight. Joint portraits all the way, I say.

I picture you and me in Van Eyck's
Arnolfini painting. You pregnant. Or me.

Then Ruth and Yitzhak in Grant Wood's
American Gothic, her holding the fork.

Mrs Arnolfini's interior

Jan van Eyck, 1434, National Gallery, London

My husband's Seville oranges are ripening
on the window ledge; he punctures and sucks
at them before flinging the pith to the pigs.
When he's not trading silk, he likes to paint
still lifes, *natures mortes*. I know this child's
another phantom. I gather my dress under my ribs,
rest a hand where its head might be, consider names.
Soon the empiric will come, scratch *nulliparous*
with his slender feather, make a poultice
for suffocation of the womb. He says my belly is full
of pips inside a ram's head. My son's skull grew
askew in my pomegranate place, slipped out cold onto
our red sheets. My husband enjoys fine drapery and fur,
holds my hand too slackly, shows my silver wrist
scars to strangers. I've never liked him or his hats.

Daffodils

Worrying all the way home they won't bloom
I lose hope in the elevator standing next to the woman
whose dog isn't leashed and never leaves her.
They share a hair colour and a way of placing their feet
too far apart. I hold the bunch heads down as if
en route to the compactor with dead organic matter.

Worrying they'll bloom after all I let them go
against the rim of a jug from Spain I'd forgotten I had.
They are too few to cluster and loll and roll like marbles
on a plate. They've got the necks of wading birds
turning to peck. Or sulk. I set the jug on my desk
expecting to wait a day as you must for certain fruit.

Worrying I've put too much faith in a flowering
I start a letter to my mother who likes flowers but
never buys them. I'm busy not telling her the damage
is almost undone, that I'm ready for mothering myself
when there's a crack—a bud has split its onionskin dress
and I shudder like an eavesdropper, sick with luck.

Frozen dream

I choose him because he likes Rembrandt,
redwoods, once kept a guinea pig;

you choose him because he can't dance,
writes neatly, listens to Patsy Cline.

The website has his photo at two.
I think bushbaby; you think owl.

It's against the odds, I say.
Like rolling a six. Twice.

You tell me my luck's increased with age,
cite my recent success at scissors/paper/stone.

At the clinic a take-home vial in a tank.
DO NOT THAW UNTIL NEEDED.

I grip him tightly between my knees all the way
back from Cortlandt to 8th,

hand-hold him up Broadway like a toddler.
Those eyes of his are everywhere.

It's snowing and I want to serve a proper meal
for once, set the table nice

but I slip into church, make him
sit through some kind of silent marriage;

flick-read a flypaper Bible, stopping at will.
It says *Luke*. A solid name but not right.

An earnest search of the hymnal yields
Before The Ending of the Day. English/French.

It says he likes to cook, bake, work with his hands.
I head home, scared of my own oven.

chicken

my father would often drive us towards oncoming traffic
this hits me in the still alone of the recovery room
where nothing's oncoming now except sharing the bad news
the anaesthetist arrives to check my pain level isn't ten
it's seven i say meaning four or five but wanting fentanyl
even more urgently than the persimmon (like cantaloupe but
more sour) i'd craved before i'd even had one—
exactly the type of blind faith involved in wanting this child
also needed while being driven at high speed in the wrong lane
unable to surrender like a floppy baby rag doll
reliant instead on taut prayer to saints—probably francis
kind to animals (unlike my father who threw
our pet bird against a wall) in a game i've called
someone has to die aka *who is the most scared*—
all the impact of his own death-dread lodged in my body
which is why i'm in a hurry and have left it so late and
against the odds— the same reasons he said
he would often drive us towards oncoming traffic

frozen embryo:

day one: *light and dark:* a lit dish: a piercing: unseen division: a before and after: **day two:** *water and sky:* suspension: flux: gather: fluidity: solution: **day three:** *plants and land:* footing: substance: burgeon: a mattering: **day four:** *sun and moon:* gleam: ritual: affinity: a redoubling: **day five:** *fish and birds:* flutter: nestle: press: a teeming: **day six:** *animals and humans:* dominion: semblance: naming: gender: splitting: **day seven:** *rest*

undead as a girl

our doctor in her blue scrubs
clean cotton warmth

pressed against my thighs
a woman impregnating me

i swallow laughter like it's church
can't think of anything more divine

i had miscarried my gender
so i could live in my own body

i had miscarried my body
so i could live in my own gender

our doctor in her white coat
says she can tell the sex

there's your heart
its translucence an honesty

i feel you quicken inside me
become undead as a girl

Finding Rapa Nui on Google Earth (May, 2020)

'Easter Island where everything is an altar' – Pablo Neruda

When I can't sleep for the pandemonium
I leave my body: the contagion of my own anxiety,

the fragile liquid microverse of my pregnancy.
I want to go where the worst has already happened.

My watery screen-world spins and tilts;
the Earth slows, stops, zooms.

This land is pocked with things made
then broken; stone bodies are strewn.

A thin mane of wild horses runs across
the caldera out of anyone's control: a family,

all febrile leg blur. I envy them.
On the headland, boys stand side-by-side

preparing to sea-dive in unison,
their unspoken alignment an archetype.

On a cliff an etched tern offers up
its single egg: the manutara, lucky bird.

I want to leave without touching or taking,
make the world turn again, go back

to my brash mercantile city asleep
in its locked-down gridded quiet.

The half-buried moai with their absent eyes
are like me—in it up to their necks.

My unborn baby kicks
and, like a blinking cursor, locates itself.

Confinement

April 2020; for my wife

The lending of your soft shirt
when our baby pushes me out of my seams
and into the cotton of yours.
Blue plaid worn thin by the frictions of your skin.
You lifting it off, three buttons already undone,
me thinking how our baby will soon be pulled free of me.
My teeth and breath at your shoulder blade, you laying me
down, the new borders of my body keeping us distant,
pressing other parts closer than before this makeshift shape.
Then because I couldn't go outside, you saw the spring
flowers without me, came home describing the colours,
how you'd touched a pink petal. You laid a hand
on my stomach and said without covering anything up
you are the cherry blossom, and I smiled at our ordinary
and out of the ordinary inside love.

recovery

i love your given-up drunkenness
how the cravings have switched to me

your desire shows up like adrenaline
quick blood to muscle, dilation

when we message it's emergency
your words allruntogether

i am listening to johnnycash you will say
or iambakingbread, comehomenow

you always want me like surgery
several quick procedures
then a long complex intervention

i've learned to do triage
attend selectively
make most of your body wait

sometimes you tell me your dreams:
a no walls house, white
basement inundated, unsafe for mortgage

in the morning you slice an apple
eat it off the blade
ask if i'm going to write about you

if you do, you say, make me perfect
make me perfect please

settled

and afterwards
the fact that
you think nothing of
going about the house
naked under my bedcover
and finding me busy with
kitchen things
smile
before towing your soft cloak
sibilantly
along the hall
to the next room
where you sit
in the middle of the floor
in the middle of the day
laughing at an old cartoon
with our atmosphere
spread around you
like a monument
makes me wonder why
i ever settled
for anything less

ultrasound / ego gravida

in response to the 'botched' Ecce Homo *fresco, Borja*

i see my baby every four weeks
in between times i imagine her face

my chiaroscuro view of her red world
is a limited engagement, museum hours

i seem to leave without her every time
even though she's still inside me, amniotic.

this time my baby's ears have moved into place
soft palate for swallowing, lips for sucking

i feel like the woman who overpainted jesus
kept giving him new features

her secret brushing a protection
against a shared crisis of flake and craquelure.

one day she left his mouth wide open
in the urgent pose of a hungry doll

forgot the fleck of white in his pupils
painted the life right out of him

i heard that trees fruit because they're dying
ego gravida: i am laden, great with child.

you were no oil painting, says my mother
recalling my newborn look and i realise

motherhood is about surviving our own
deadness, others' aliveness, and vice versa.

free association

my interior life began with the silent naming of my orange plastic bathtime boat. twice a week i nudged *afternoon sunshine* to safe harbour through fairy liquid foam. my mother used to get up for the lunchtime news—*afternoon sunshine* she'd say squinting at the tv with lit cigarette. for attention i tried singing 'bright eyes' outside the kitchen door but made only myself cry. i am the daughter of circus performers and steel workers. they have in common flying knives. i was born in the year of the pig and decimalisation, arrived like a new currency—cold, strange to the touch, something to be studied, turned over in the hand. our council estate's streets had famous college names: corpus christi close was an ongoing joke. my father always made me feel like the remote-controlled planes he kept building and crashing. one day on a visit to freud's house with the afternoon sunshine streaming in i wanted to sit down on the thick carpet and never leave. his houseplants are still growing through careful propagation, which is why i sit in a soft chair tending to the hurt places i never had tended—one of many janus-faced joys of being a psychoanalyst poet. the others all involve naming boats.

ACKNOWLEDGEMENTS

Poems in this pamphlet have been selected in competitions including the Rialto Nature and Place Poetry Competition ('Daffodils' appeared in *Rialto* 93), the Live Canon International Poem Competition, and the 2020 Fish International Poetry Competition, judged by Billy Collins. A previous version of this pamphlet was shortlisted for the 2019 Rialto Pamphlet Competition.

༄

Thank you to my dear friends and earliest readers of these poems: Nikki Chesterman, Jeremy Pollet, Donna Prenta, Columba Quigley, Susan Schulman, and Jude Shaw.

Thank you to my wonderful poetry mentor, Heidi Williamson, and my academic mentor and wise friend, Dr Celia Hunt.

I'm grateful to my editor, the starlike Emma Wright, for her sure touch and creative energy.

I've drawn inspiration from tutors and students on courses at The Poetry School UK, during which many of these poems were written.

Thank you to my clinical supervisors at the National Institute for the Psychotherapies in New York City who encouraged this part of me.

Deep gratitude to Anna Alward, Mary Ellen McMahon and Bonnie Zindel, who helped heal the roots so the tree could blossom.

Finally, to my psychotherapy patients (past, present, and future), thank you for the example of your courage, and our richness of relationship.

ABOUT THE POET

Rachael Matthews was born in Chesterfield, Derbyshire, and grew up in her grandmother's seaside B&B and in social housing in Great Yarmouth, Norfolk. A former national BBC Radio journalist and newsreader, she retrained as a psychoanalytic psychotherapist via an MA in Creative Writing and a PhD at Sussex University, exploring trauma and creativity. She has lived in New York for more than a decade, and has worked there as a clinician at a non-profit therapy centre for the past several years. She also facilitates expressive writing groups for seniors and those experiencing homelessness and addiction recovery. She is working on her first collection.

Rachael won The Beach Hut's Coastal Writing for Wellness Competition in 2020 and has twice been a runner up in the Mslexia Poetry Competition, which was judged by Kathleen Jamie and Carol Ann Duffy. She came third in the 2020 Magma Poetry Competition judged by Caroline Bird, and one of her poems was chosen for the Poetry School's celebration of Poem in Your Pocket Day. Her poems have been anthologised by Cinnamon Press and Templar Poetry, and published in the journal *Psychoanalytic Perspectives* (Taylor & Francis) and *Writing on the Moon: Stories and Poetry from the Creative Unconscious by Psychoanalysts and Others* (Routledge, 2017).

ABOUT THE EMMA PRESS

The Emma Press is an independent publisher based in Birmingham, UK, and dedicated to producing beautiful books for adults and children. In 2020 The Emma Press was awarded funding from Arts Council England as part of the Elevate programme.